Komodo Dragon

The World's Biggest Lizard

by Natalie Lunis

Consultants:

Claudio Ciofi, Ph.D.
Department of Animal Biology and Genetics
University of Florence, Italy
and Research Affiliate, Yale University, USA

Meredith Whitney
Herpetology and Conservation Manager
The Maryland Zoo in Baltimore
Baltimore, MD

BEARPORT
PUBLISHING

New York, New York

Credits

Cover, ©Jim Blake/Shutterstock; 2–3, ©Brandon Seidel/Shutterstock; 4, Kathrin Ayer; 4–5, ©Cyril Ruoso/JH Editorial/
Minden Pictures; 6, ©Adrian T. Jones/Shutterstock; 7BKG, ©Cyril Ruoso/JH Editorial/Minden Pictures; 8, ©Stan Osolinski/
Oxford Scientific; 9, ©James Kern Expeditions; 10, ©Toby Sinclair/Nature Picture Library; 11, ©Conrad Maufe/Nature
Picture Library; 12 (inset), ©Cyril Ruoso/JH Editorial/Minden Pictures; 12–13, ©B. Jones and M. Shimlock/NHPA; 14–15,
©Tui de Roy/Minden Pictures; 16 (inset), ©Michael Pitts/Minden Pictures; 16–17, ©Michael Pitts/Minden Pictures; 18,
©James Kern Expeditions; 19, ©Cyril Ruoso/JH Editorial/Minden Pictures; 20–21, ©Cyril Ruoso/JH Editorial/Minden
Pictures; 22L, ©Conrad Maufe/Nature Picture Library; 22C, ©Claus Meyer/Minden Pictures; 22R, ©Fred Bruemme/Peter
Arnold; 23TL, ©Bill Love/NHPA; 23TR, ©Michael Pitts/Minden Pictures; 23BL, ©Boyd Norton; 23BR, ©Geoff Higgins/
Oxford Scientific; 23BKG, ©Patrick Faggot/NHPA.

Publisher: Kenn Goin
Editorial Director: Adam Siegel
Editorial Development: Nancy Hall, Inc.
Creative Director: Spencer Brinker
Photo Researcher: Carousel Research, Inc.: Mary Teresa Giancoli
Design: Otto Carbajal

Library of Congress Cataloging-in-Publication Data

Lunis, Natalie.
 Komodo dragon : the world's biggest lizard / by Natalie Lunis.
     p. cm.—(SuperSized!)
 Includes bibliographical references and index.
 ISBN-13: 978-1-59716-392-7 (library binding)
 ISBN-10: 1-59716-392-9 (library binding)
 1. Komodo dragon—Juvenile literature. I. Title.

QL666.L29L86 2007
597.95'968—dc22

                    2006031853

For more information, write to Bearport Publishing Company, Inc., 101 Fifth Avenue,
Suite 6R, New York, New York 10003. Printed in the United States of America.

10 9 8 7 6 5 4 3 2 1

Contents

A Big Lizard

The Komodo dragon is the biggest lizard in the world.

A Komodo dragon is longer than most large surfboards.

A Komodo dragon can grow up to 10 feet (3 m) long. It can weigh up to 300 pounds (136 kg).

Island Homes

Komodo dragons live on a few islands in Indonesia.

They spend most of their time in forests and **grasslands**.

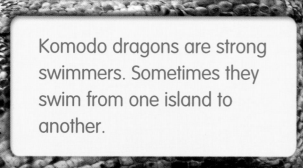

Komodo dragons are strong swimmers. Sometimes they swim from one island to another.

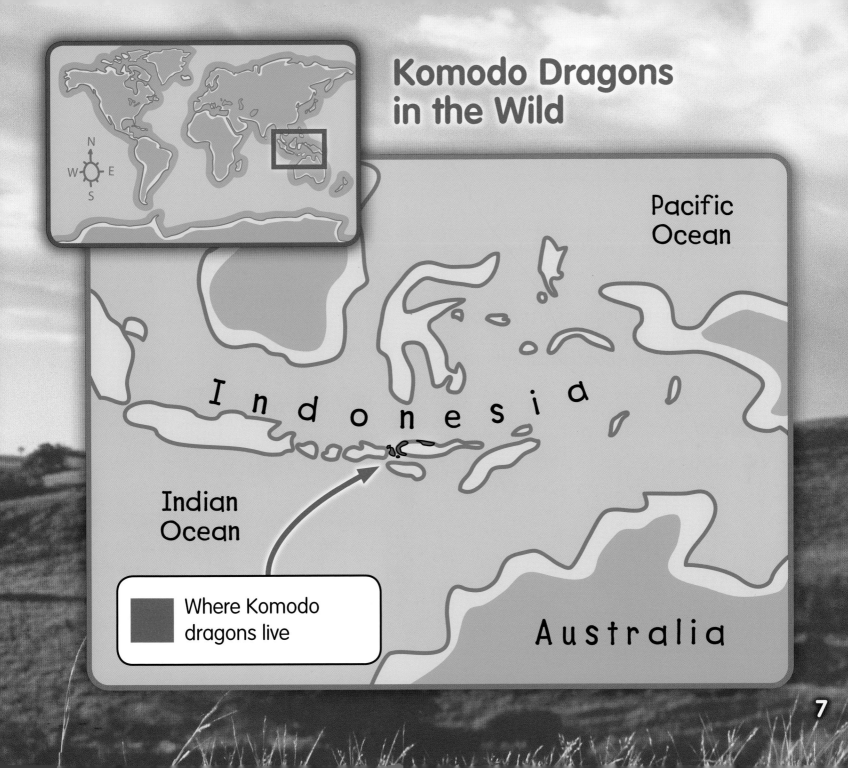

Komodo Dragons in the Wild

Pacific Ocean

Indonesia

Indian Ocean

Where Komodo dragons live

Australia

A Tongue That Can Smell

Komodo dragons have long, forked tongues.

They flick their tongues in and out.

As they do, they pick up smells in the air.

The smells help them track down their food.

Using its tongue, a Komodo dragon can smell food up to 5 miles (8 km) away.

tongue

What's for Dinner?

Komodo dragons will eat any kind of meat.

They find and eat the rotting bodies of dead animals.

They also hunt both large and small animals.

Some of the bigger animals they hunt are wild pigs, deer, goats, and **water buffalo**.

water buffalo

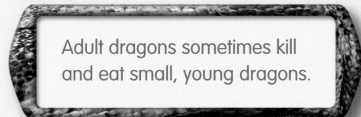

Adult dragons sometimes kill and eat small, young dragons.

Big Bites

A Komodo dragon does not chew its food.

Instead, it tears big chunks of meat from a dead animal.

It opens its jaws wide.

Then it can swallow a chunk of food bigger than its own head.

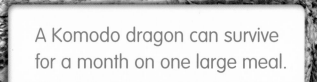

A Komodo dragon can survive for a month on one large meal.

A Cozy Nest

Komodo dragons hatch from eggs.

A female digs a hole and lays up to 30 eggs in it.

Then she covers the nest with dirt to protect it.

She usually does not stay behind to take care of the eggs.

Komodo dragon eggs are about 3 inches (7.6 cm) long. Their shells are tough and leathery.

Little Lizards

The dragon eggs hatch after about eight months.

The **hatchlings** are around 18 inches (46 cm) long.

They climb up trees and eat insects, **geckos**, and birds.

The little lizards live in the trees for the first two years of their lives.

Komodo dragons live up to 50 years.

hatchling

Staying Alive

Living in trees helps young dragons escape their enemies.

They try to stay away from snakes, wild dogs, and hungry adult dragons.

After two years, the young dragons are almost as big as the adults.

At last it is safe enough to come down and live on the ground.

young dragon

Adult dragons are too big to climb trees. If they try to climb up, they fall to the ground.

Dragon Tales

Many fairy tales are about dragons.

Yet there is a big difference between dragons in stories and Komodo dragons.

The fairy-tale dragons are make-believe.

Komodo dragons are real!

The big lizards may have been called dragons because of their forked tongues. When the lizards flicked them, they looked like fire-breathing dragons to some people.

Index

Read More

Darling, Kathy. *Komodo Dragon: On Location.* New York: HarperCollins Children's Books (1997).

Kalman, Bobbie. *Endangered Komodo Dragons.* New York: Crabtree Publishing Company (2004).

Miller, Jake. *The Komodo Dragon.* New York: PowerKids Press (2003).

Learn More Online

To learn more about Komodo dragons, visit **www.bearportpublishing.com/SuperSized**